Juicing For Beginners

1500 Days of Juicing Recipes to Detox Your Body, Boost Your Energy and Lose Weight in an Easy and Natural Way

ANGELA GREEN

TABLE OF CONTENTS

Conclusion 71

Introduction

Juicing has become increasingly popular in recent years as a way to improve overall health and wellness. The process of extracting juice from fruits and vegetables allows for a concentrated dose of nutrients and enzymes that can be easily absorbed by the body. Not only is juicing a convenient way to consume a large variety of fruits and vegetables, but it also allows for experimentation with unique flavor combinations.

In this recipe book, we will explore the many benefits of juicing and provide delicious and easy-to-follow recipes for you to try at home. Whether you are new to juicing or have been doing it for years, there is something for everyone in this book. From classic juice combinations to more unique and exotic blends, we have curated a collection of recipes that will excite your taste buds and support your overall health.

Juicing can be a powerful tool for weight loss, improved digestion, increased energy levels, and even disease prevention. The high levels of vitamins, minerals, and antioxidants found in fruits and vegetables can help to strengthen the immune system and protect against a variety of chronic diseases. Additionally, juicing can be a great way to detoxify the body and improve skin health.

In this book, we will also discuss the various types of juicers available on the market and the pros and cons of each one. We will also provide tips and tricks for selecting the freshest produce and storing your juice to ensure maximum nutrient retention.

We hope that this recipe book will inspire you to incorporate juicing into your daily routine and experience the many benefits it has to offer. So, grab your juicer, and let's get started on a journey to better health and delicious juice combinations!

Benefits of Juicing

Juicing has become a popular trend in recent years, and for good reason. The process of extracting juice from fruits and vegetables allows for a concentrated dose of nutrients and enzymes that can be easily absorbed by the body. Juicing has a wide range of benefits, including weight loss, improved digestion, increased energy levels, and even disease prevention.

One of the most obvious benefits of juicing is weight loss. Juicing allows you to consume a large variety of fruits and vegetables in a convenient and easy-to-digest form. This can help to curb hunger and reduce overall calorie intake. Additionally, many fruits and vegetables are high in fiber, which helps to keep you feeling full and satisfied.

Juicing can also improve digestion. When you juice fruits and vegetables, you are removing the pulp and fibers, which can make it easier for the body to digest. This can be particularly beneficial for individuals who have trouble digesting raw fruits and vegetables. The high levels of enzymes found in fresh juice can also aid in the digestion process.

Another benefit of juicing is increased energy levels. The high levels of vitamins, minerals, and antioxidants found in fruits and vegetables can help to boost the immune system and provide the body with the necessary nutrients to function at its best. Additionally, many fruits and vegetables are high in electrolytes, which can help to keep the body hydrated and energized.

Juicing can also be a powerful tool for disease prevention. The high levels of vitamins, minerals, and antioxidants found in fruits and vegetables can help to strengthen the immune system and protect against a variety of chronic diseases, including heart disease, cancer, and diabetes. Additionally, many fruits and vegetables contain phytochemicals, which have been shown to have anti-inflammatory and anti-cancer properties.

Juicing can also be a great way to detoxify the body and improve skin health. The high levels of vitamins, minerals, and antioxidants found in fruits and vegetables can help to flush toxins out of the body, which can improve the overall health and appearance of the skin. Additionally, many fruits and vegetables contain high levels of vitamin C, which is essential for collagen production and the maintenance of healthy skin.

In addition to the above benefits, juicing is also a great way to increase your intake of fruits and vegetables. Many people struggle to consume the recommended daily amount of fruits and vegetables, and juicing is a convenient and delicious way to do so. Additionally, juicing allows for experimentation with unique flavor combinations, which can make consuming fruits and vegetables more enjoyable.

Juicing can have a wide range of benefits for overall health and wellness. It can aid in weight loss, improve digestion, increase energy levels, and even disease prevention. Additionally, juicing is a convenient and delicious way to increase your intake of fruits and vegetables and experiment with unique flavor combinations.

In summary, juicing can have several benefits for overall health and well-being. Here is a list of some of its benefits:

- Increased nutrient intake: Juicing allows you to easily consume a large number of fruits and vegetables in one glass, providing your body with a variety of essential vitamins, minerals, and phytochemicals.

- Improved digestion: Drinking juice can be easier on the digestive system, as the body does not have to work as hard to break down the food. This can be especially beneficial for those with digestive issues.

- Weight loss: Juicing can be a low-calorie way to consume a large number of nutrients, and can help with weight loss.

Detoxifying: Juicing can help flush toxins out of the body and support the liver's natural detoxification process.

Boosted Immune System: Consuming fruits and vegetables that are high in Vitamin C and antioxidants can help boost the immune system, helping to fight off infections and illnesses.

Mental Clarity: Certain fruits and vegetables contain compounds that can help improve brain function, enhance mood and boost mental clarity.

Making Your Juice

Making your juice at home is a simple and rewarding process that allows you to control the ingredients and ensure the freshness of your juice. There are a few things to keep in mind when making your juice, including the type of product to use, the equipment needed, and the proper storage of your juice.

The first thing to consider when making your juice is the type of product to use. It's best to use fresh, organic fruits and vegetables that are in season. These will have the highest nutrient content and will provide the best flavor. When selecting produce, look for fruits and vegetables that are firm and free from blemishes or damage. It's also important to wash your produce thoroughly before juicing to remove any dirt or pesticides.

The next thing to consider when making your juice is the equipment needed. There are several types of juicers available on the market, including centrifugal juicers, masticating juicers, and triturating juicers. Centrifugal juicers are the most common and affordable type,

they use a fast-spinning blade to extract the juice and they are best for juicing hard fruits and vegetables. Masticating juicers use a slow-moving auger to extract the juice and they are best for juicing leafy greens and soft fruits. Triturating juicers use both a slow-moving auger and a high-pressure press to extract the juice and they are the most efficient and versatile type of juicer.

When making your juice, it's important to follow the manufacturer's instructions for your specific juicer. This will ensure that you are getting the most juice possible and that you are not damaging the machine.

Once you have your juice, it's important to store it properly to ensure maximum freshness and nutrient retention. Juice should be stored in an airtight container and kept in the refrigerator. It's best to consume the juice within 24 hours of juicing to ensure maximum freshness, however, it can last up to 72 hours if stored properly.

Making your juice at home is a simple and rewarding process that allows you to control the ingredients and ensure the freshness of your juice. It's important to use fresh, organic fruits and vegetables that are in season and to properly clean your produce before juicing. The equipment needed will depend on the type of product you're juicing and your budget, also it's important to follow the manufacturer's instructions for your specific juicer. Once you have your juice, it's important to store it properly to ensure maximum freshness and

nutrient retention. With a little bit of knowledge and the right equipment, you can enjoy the many benefits of homemade juice.

Necessary Precautions:

Juicing is a popular and healthy way to consume a large variety of fruits and vegetables, however, some precautions should be taken to ensure safety and the best results. Here are some important precautions to keep in mind while juicing:

- Cleanliness: It's important to clean your juicer, produce, and utensils thoroughly before juicing to prevent the spread of bacteria. This will ensure that your juice is safe to consume and will also help to prolong the life of your juicer.

- Allergies: If you have any food allergies, it's important to be aware of the ingredients in your juice and

10

to avoid any ingredients that may cause an allergic reaction. It's also important to be aware of the potential cross-contamination of allergens, such as if you are making juice in the same juicer that you have used previously to juice nuts.

- Oxidation: Juice can become oxidized quickly, which can reduce the nutrient content and change the taste of the juice. To prevent oxidation, it's important to consume your juice as soon as possible after juicing and to store it in an airtight container in the refrigerator.

- Over-Juicing: Consuming too much juice can lead to an excessive intake of sugar and can cause diarrhea. Juice should be consumed in moderation and should be considered as a supplement to a well-balanced diet, not as a meal replacement. It's also important to

be aware of the sugar content of fruits and vegetables, such as carrots and beets, that are high in natural sugars.

- Interactions with Medication: Some fruits and vegetables, such as grapefruit, may interact with certain medications and may affect their effectiveness. It's important to be aware of any potential interactions and to consult with your healthcare provider if you have any concerns.

- High-Speed Juicers: Some juicers, like centrifugal juicers, use high speeds to extract juice, which can generate heat. This can cause the juice to lose some of its nutrient content and can also change the taste of the juice. To prevent this, it's important to use a low-speed juicer or to consume the juice as soon as possible after juicing.

- Use of pesticides: It's important to use organic fruits and vegetables whenever possible to avoid consuming pesticides. If organic produce is not available, it's important to wash your produce thoroughly before juicing to remove any dirt or pesticides.

By following these precautions, you can ensure the safety and quality of your juice and maximize the health benefits. Juicing is a great way to consume a large variety of fruits and vegetables and can be a powerful tool for overall health and wellness, but it's important to do it safely and responsibly.

Breakfast Juices

Orange Carrot Juice

Orange Carrot Juice is a delicious and refreshing juice that is packed with vitamins and nutrients. This recipe is a great way to start your day or to enjoy it as a healthy snack. The combination of sweet oranges and earthy carrots creates a perfect balance of flavors and the addition of ginger gives it a little kick of spice. Not only is it delicious but it's also very easy to make and requires only a few simple ingredients. This juice is perfect for those looking to improve their digestion, boost their immune system, and get a healthy dose of vitamins and minerals.

Ingredients:

- 4 oranges

- 3 carrots

Instructions:

- Peel and chop the oranges and carrots.
- Juice the oranges and carrots in a juicer.
- Serve immediately.

Apple Ginger Juice

Introducing our delicious Apple Ginger Juice recipe! This refreshing and healthy juice is made with fresh apples and ginger, making it a perfect combination of sweet and spicy flavors. With its high level of antioxidants and anti-inflammatory properties, this juice is great for boosting the immune system and promoting overall health and wellness.

Ingredients

- 2 apples
- 1-inch piece of ginger

Instructions:

- Peel and chop the apples and ginger.
- Juice the apples and ginger in a juicer.
- Serve immediately.

Pineapple Kale Juice

This refreshing and nutrient-packed juice is made with fresh pineapple and kale, providing a perfect balance of sweet and bitter flavors. This recipe is easy to make and is packed with vitamins, minerals, and antioxidants. Perfect for a morning boost or a post-workout refreshment. This recipe is simple, healthy, and delicious. Give it a try!

Ingredients:

- 1 cup of pineapple chunks,
- 2 cups of kale

Instructions:

- Wash and chop the pineapple and kale.
- Juice the pineapple and kale in a juicer.
- Serve immediately.

Strawberry Spinach Juice

This Strawberry Spinach Juice recipe is a delicious and nutritious blend of sweet strawberries and nutrient-rich spinach. It's a perfect way to start your day or to enjoy a refreshing afternoon pick-me-up. This recipe is easy to make and requires only a few simple ingredients. With its bright and vibrant color, it's not only good for you but also pleasing to the eye.

Get your juicer ready and let's make some juice!

Ingredients:

1 cup of strawberries

2 cups of spinach

Instructions:

- Rinse and chop the strawberries and spinach.
- Juice the strawberries and spinach in a juicer.
- Serve immediately.

Cucumber Lime Juice

This Cucumber Lime Juice recipe is a refreshing and healthy combination of cucumber and lime. The cucumber provides hydration and a cool, crisp taste while the lime adds a burst of citrus flavor and a boost of vitamin C. This juice is easy to make and

perfect for a hot summer day or to enjoy any time of the year as a healthy and delicious drink.

Ingredients:

- 1 cucumber
- 1 lime

Instructions:

- Peel and chop the cucumber and lime.
- Juice the cucumber and lime in a juicer.
- Serve immediately.

Mango Blueberry Juice

This Mango Blueberry Juice recipe is a delicious and nutritious blend of sweet and tangy flavors. Made with fresh mangos and blueberries, this juice is a great way to start your day or refresh yourself during a hot summer day. It's a simple recipe that requires only a few ingredients and a juicer. With its high levels of vitamins, minerals, and antioxidants, this juice is sure to boost your energy levels and leave you feeling refreshed.

Ingredients:

- 1 Mango
- 1 cup of blueberries

Instructions:

- Peel and chop the Mango, Rinse the blueberries.
- Juice the Mango and blueberries in a juicer.
- Serve immediately.

Beet, Apple and Carrot Juice

This vibrant blend combines the earthy sweetness of beets with the crispness of apples and the sweetness of carrots to create a juice that is not only delicious but also packed with vitamins and minerals. This recipe is perfect for a morning boost or as a post-workout pick-me-up. Give it a try and feel the benefits of this healthy and tasty juice. "

Ingredients:

- 2 medium beets
- 2 apples
- 2 carrots

Instructions:

- Peel and chop the beets, apples, and carrots.
- Juice the beets, apples, and carrots in a juicer.
- Serve immediately.

Green Juice

Green juice is a delicious and nutritious way to boost your intake of fruits and vegetables. Made with a combination of leafy greens and other nutrient-rich ingredients, green juice is a quick and easy way to get a concentrated dose of vitamins, minerals, and antioxidants. This recipe is perfect for anyone looking to improve their overall health and wellness.

Ingredients:

- 2 cups of spinach
- 1 cup of kale
- ½ a cucumber
- ½ a lemon

Instructions:

- Spinach, kale, cucumber, and lemon should all be washed and chopped.
- Use a juicer to extract the juice from the components.
- Serve immediately.

Carrot Apple Juice

Carrot Apple Juice is a delicious and nutritious combination of two of the healthiest foods in the world. This juice is easy to make and packed with vitamins, minerals, and antioxidants that will help to improve your overall health and wellness. The sweetness of the apple pairs perfectly with the earthy taste of the carrots, making for a balanced and satisfying juice that is sure to please the palate. So, grab your juicer, and let's get started on making a refreshing and healthy Carrot Apple Juice!

Ingredients:

- 4 medium-sized carrots,
- 2 apples

Instructions:

- Obtain some apples and carrots, then prep them by peeling and chopping them.

- The apples and carrots should be juiced.
- Serve immediately.

Grapefruit and Ginger Juice

This Grapefruit and Ginger Juice recipe is a refreshing and healthy option that combines the tangy flavor of grapefruit with the warming properties of ginger. The ginger adds a spicy kick and also has anti-inflammatory properties, while the grapefruit is high in Vitamin C and helps in digestion. This recipe is perfect for a morning boost or as a post-workout drink. This recipe is easy to make and can be enjoyed both fresh and cold.

Ingredients:

- 2 grapefruits
- 1-inch piece of ginger

Instructions:

- Peel the grapefruits and ginger and cut them up.
- Use a juicer to get the juice from the grapefruit and ginger.
- Serve right away.

Pumpkin Juice

Pumpkin Juice is a delicious and healthy way to enjoy the flavors of fall. Made with fresh pumpkin puree, spices, and sweetener, this juice is perfect for sipping on a cool autumn day. With a rich pumpkin flavor, this juice is also packed with vitamins and minerals, making it a great addition to a well-balanced diet. Whether you're looking for a healthy snack or a festive drink, this pumpkin juice recipe is sure to please.

Ingredients:

- 6 carrots
- 2 sweet potatoes

- 2 squash
- 1 cup diced pumpkin

Instructions:

- Use a juicer to make juice from the carrots, sweet potatoes, squash, and pumpkin.
- Stir well to mix the ingredients.

Ginger Apple Fizz

This recipe combines the zesty flavor of ginger with the sweetness of apples and a hint of fizz for a unique and invigorating juice. Perfect for a morning pick-me-up or a post-workout thirst quencher, this juice is packed with vitamins, minerals, and antioxidants to support your overall health and well-being. So, grab your juicer, and let's get started on making this delicious and healthy juice!

Ingredients:

- 1 pear

- 2 apples
- 2 ounces seltzer water

Instructions:

- Use a juicer to process the ginger, then the pears and apples.
- Pour the seltzer into the juice and mix it well.

Ginger Tea

Ginger tea is a delicious and healthy beverage that has many benefits. It is easy to make and can be enjoyed hot or cold. This ginger tea juice recipe is a simple and refreshing way to enjoy the benefits of ginger. It's a perfect drink to enjoy any time of day and is great for soothing an upset stomach or boosting the immune system.

Ingredients:

- 4 cups water
- 2-inch piece ginger
- ¼ lemon

- Let the water boil, then add the ginger.

- Let boil for 15 to 20 minutes.

- Put the ginger in the trash and strain the tea.

- Squeeze in lemon juice to taste.

Citrus Sparkler

"Refresh your taste buds with this Citrus Sparkler Juice recipe. This delicious blend of oranges, lemons, and limes is the perfect combination of sweet and tangy. The added ginger gives it a hint of spice and added health benefits. This easy-to-make recipe is perfect for any time of the day, and it's a great way to incorporate more citrus fruits into your diet. Get your juicer ready and let's get started!"

Ingredients:

- ¼ pineapple

- 1 orange

- 1 lemon

- 2 ounces seltzer water

Instructions:

- Put the pineapple, lemon, and orange in a juicer, and then add the seltzer.

- Give it a good stir to mix.

Green Meanie

Introducing the Green Meanie Juice, a delicious and nutritious blend of leafy greens, cucumber, and ginger. This juice is packed with vitamins, minerals, and antioxidants, making it the perfect way to start your day or refuel after a workout. It's a great way to get your daily dose of greens and boost your immune system. The ginger adds a spicy kick that makes this juice even more refreshing. Give it a try and you will love it!

Ingredients:

- 1 cup spinach
- 4 kale leaves
- 6 Brussels sprouts
- 2 green onions with stalks
- 1 jalapeño pepper
- 2 garlic cloves
- 1 lime
- 1 cucumber

Instructions:

- Use a juicer to blend the spinach, kale, Brussels sprouts, and green onions.
- Then blend the jalapeno, garlic, lime, and cucumber. Mix well to blend.

Pomegranate Cherry Juice

This Pomegranate Cherry Juice recipe is a delicious and healthy blend of antioxidant-rich pomegranate and sweet cherries. This juice is easy to make and packed with vitamins, minerals, and antioxidants. Perfect for a refreshing morning drink or a post-workout boost, this recipe is sure to become a staple in your juicing routine.

Ingredients:

- 2 beets
- ½ cup blackberries
- 1 pomegranate (or substitute 1 cup of cranberries)
- ½ cup sour cherries
- 2 kiwis

Instructions:

- Use a juicer to make juice from the beets and blackberries, then the pomegranate, cherries, and kiwis.
- Give it a good stir to mix.

Apple Mint Juice

This Apple Mint Juice recipe is a refreshing and healthy blend of crisp apples and refreshing mint.

It's easy to make and packed with vitamins and antioxidants. The combination of sweet apples and mint creates a delicious and invigorating flavor that is perfect for any time of the day. The perfect juice to boost your energy and refresh your breath. Give it a try!

Ingredients:

- 4 mint sprigs
- 2 apples
- 1 carrot
- 1 pear
- 2 kiwis

Instructions

- Use a juicer to process the mint, then the apples, carrots, and pears, and finally the kiwis.
- Give it a good stir to mix.

Cherry Berry Mint Julep

Introducing our delicious Cherry Berry Mint Julep Juice recipe, a refreshing and healthy blend of cherries, mixed berries, mint, and lime juice. This juice is packed with antioxidants, vitamins, and minerals, making it a perfect start to your day or a refreshing pick-me-up any time of the day. The combination of sweet and tart flavors makes for a delicious and satisfying drink that's sure to please. Get ready to enjoy this tasty and healthy juice recipe!

Ingredients:

- 4 mint sprigs
- 1 cup cherries
- 1 cup raspberries
- 1 cucumber
- 1 apple

Instructions:

- Use a juicer to process the mint, then the cherries and raspberries, then the cucumber and apple.
- Give it a good stir to mix.

Pineapple Cherry Punch

Introducing our delicious Pineapple Cherry Punch Juice recipe! This refreshing juice is the perfect combination of sweet pineapple and tart cherry. This recipe is easy to make and packed with vitamins, minerals, and antioxidants. Perfect for a morning pick-me-up or a post-workout refreshment. So, grab your juicer, and let's get started on making this delicious and nutritious juice!

Ingredients:

- ¼ pineapple
- 2 plums
- 1 cup sour cherries

Instructions:

- Put all the ingredients through a juicer and mix them well.

Spicy Lemonade

This Spicy Lemonade Juice recipe is the perfect blend of sweet and tangy with a kick of heat. It's a refreshing and healthy way to enjoy the summer season. Made with fresh lemons, sugar, water, and a touch of cayenne pepper, this juice is sure to wake up your taste buds and leave you feeling energized. Perfect to enjoy on a hot summer day or as a morning detox drink. Give it a try and get ready to be surprised by the delicious taste of this spicy lemonade juice!

Ingredients:

- 3 lemons
- 1 cucumber
- 1 cup water
- ½ teaspoon cayenne pepper

Instructions:

- Use a juicer to process the lemons and cucumbers.

- Mix the water and cayenne pepper well into the juice.

Meal Replacement Smoothie

Mango, Spinach and Avocado Smoothie

This recipe is for a delicious and nutritious smoothie made with ripe mango, spinach, and avocado. The sweet mango provides a natural sweetness, while the spinach and avocado add a boost of vitamins and healthy fats. This smoothie is perfect as a breakfast or a post-workout drink. It's easy to make and packed with flavor and nutrients, making it a great way to start your day or refuel after a workout.

Ingredients:

- 1½ cups 100% original coconut water
- 1 cup fresh or frozen mango pieces
- 2 cups baby spinach leaves
- ½ ripe, Fresh California Avocado, seeded, peeled, and cubed
- 1 scoop vanilla protein powder (whey, soy, pea, or rice)

Instructions:

- Pour the coconut water into a blender, then add the rest of the ingredients.
- Mix until it's smooth.

Creamy Cinnamon, Carrot, Orange and Avocado Smoothie

Introducing our Creamy Cinnamon, Carrot, Orange, and Avocado Smoothie recipe, a delicious and healthy way to start your day! This smoothie is packed with healthy ingredients such as carrots and oranges for their high levels of Vitamin C, avocado for healthy fats and creaminess, and a touch of cinnamon for a warming and comforting flavor. This smoothie is easy to make and perfect for a quick breakfast or a healthy snack. Give it a try and enjoy the benefits of this nutritious and delicious recipe!

Ingredients:

- 1½ cups 100% original coconut water
- 1 cup sliced carrots
- 1 orange, peeled and cut into chunks
- ¼ tsp. ground cinnamon
- ½ ripe, Fresh California Avocado, seeded, peeled, and cubed
- 1 scoop vanilla protein powder (whey, soy, pea, or rice)

Instructions:

- Pour the coconut water into a blender, then add the rest of the ingredients.
- Mix until it's smooth.

Cool Veggie, Pineapple, and Avocado Smoothie

This recipe is for a refreshing and delicious Cool Veggie, Pineapple, and Avocado Smoothie. This smoothie is packed with nutrients and is the perfect way to start your day or refuel after a workout. With the combination of cool and creamy avocado, sweet pineapple, and nutrient-rich veggies, this smoothie will leave you feeling energized and satisfied. Give it a try and enjoy!

Ingredients:

- 1 cup 100% original coconut water
- 1 cup fresh or frozen pineapple pieces
- 1/2 cup cucumber slices
- 1-inch x ¼-inch ginger slice, peeled
- 2 cups baby spinach leaves

- 1/2 ripe, Fresh California Avocado, seeded, peeled, and cubed
- 1 scoop vanilla protein powder (whey, soy, pea, or rice)

Instructions:

- Pour the coconut water into a blender, then add the rest of the ingredients.

Blueberry, Zucchini, and California Avocado Smoothie

Introducing our Blueberry, Zucchini, and California Avocado Smoothie recipe! This unique and flavorful smoothie is a perfect blend of sweet and savory, with the added benefits of healthy fats from the avocado and a boost of vitamins and antioxidants from the blueberries and zucchini. Perfect for breakfast or as a post-workout snack.

Ingredients:

- 1 cup 100% original coconut water
- 1 cup fresh or frozen blueberries
- 1 (5-inch) zucchini, peeled and sliced
- ½ tsp. ground cinnamon
- ½ ripe, Fresh California Avocado, seeded, peeled, and cubed
- 1 scoop vanilla protein powder (whey, soy, pea, or rice)

Instructions:

- Pour the coconut water into a blender, then add the rest of the ingredients.
- Blend until smooth.

Strawberry, Watermelon, Avocado, and Mint Smoothie

Introducing our Strawberry, Watermelon, Avocado, and Mint

Smoothie recipe! This tasty and healthy smoothie is a perfect blend of sweet and refreshing flavors, with a creamy avocado texture that will be sure to delight your taste buds. Perfect for a refreshing morning or afternoon pick-me-up.

Ingredients:

- 1 cup 100% original coconut water
- 1 cup fresh or frozen strawberries, hulled
- 1 cup watermelon pieces
- 4 mint leaves
- 1/2 ripe, Fresh California Avocado, seeded, peeled, and cubed
- 1 scoop vanilla protein powder (whey, soy, pea, or rice)

Instructions:

- Pour the coconut water into a blender and then add the rest of the ingredients.
- Blend until smooth.

Almond, Banana, and Flax Smoothie

Introducing our Almond, Banana, and Flax Smoothie recipe! This nutritious and delicious smoothie is the perfect combination of creamy, nutty, and fruity flavors, perfect for breakfast or a healthy snack. It's a great way to start your day with a boost of energy!

Ingredients:

- 2 large bananas; frozen or fresh
- 1 tbsp of almond butter
- 2 tbsp of flax seeds
- ½ cup almond milk
- 1 tsp honey or maple syrup

Instructions:

- Blend all of the ingredients until they are well mixed, then serve cold.

Post-Workout Spinach, Mango, and Carrot Smoothie

Introducing our Post-Workout Spinach, Mango, and Carrot Smoothie recipe! This nutrient-dense smoothie is the perfect way to replenish your body after a workout, packed with vitamins, minerals, and antioxidants from spinach, mango, and carrot. A delicious and healthy way to recover and refuel your body.

Ingredients:

- 2 cups of spinach
- 1 cup frozen mangoes
- ½ cup baby carrots
- ½ cup plain low-fat yogurt
- ¼ cup orange juice
- ½ cup coconut water
- 2 oranges (peeled)

Instructions:

- Put all of the ingredients into a blender and blend until the mixture is smooth and creamy. Serve.

Oatmeal, Banana, and Strawberry Smoothie.

Introducing our Oatmeal, Banana, and Strawberry Smoothie recipe! This healthy and satisfying smoothie is the perfect way to start your day with a boost of energy, filled with the benefits of oatmeal, banana, and fresh strawberries.

Ingredients:

- ½ cup whole oats
- 1 cup almond milk
- 1/2 cup plain low-fat yogurt
- 2 cups frozen strawberries
- 2 ripe bananas
- 1 tbsp honey
- 1/2 tsp vanilla extract

Instructions:

- Put all of the ingredients into a blender and blend until everything is well-mixed.

Peanut Butter, Banana, and Jelly Smoothie

Introducing our Peanut Butter, Banana, and Jelly Smoothie recipe! This delicious and creamy smoothie combines the classic combination of peanut butter and jelly with the added nutrition of banana for a satisfying and flavorful breakfast or snack.

Ingredients:

- 1 ripe banana
- ½ cup almond milk
- 2 tbsp peanut butter
- 1 cup mixed frozen berries

Instructions:

- Blend until everything is smooth and creamy. Serve.

Avocado and Banana Protein Smoothie

Introducing our Avocado and Banana Protein Smoothie recipe! This creamy and nutritious smoothie is perfect for breakfast or a post-workout snack, packed with healthy fats from avocado and protein from your choice of protein powder. Enjoy the combination of avocado and banana for a delicious and satisfying smoothie.

Ingredients:

- 1 cup almond milk
- 1/3 ripe and frozen avocado
- ½ ripe banana
- ¼ cup Whey protein powder
- 1 tsp flax

Instructions:

- Add all the ingredients in a blender until well-mixed and creamy. Serve.

Coconut Milk and Blueberry Smoothie

Introducing our Coconut Milk and Blueberry Smoothie recipe! A perfect blend of creamy coconut milk and sweet blueberries, this smoothie is a delicious and healthy way to start your day.

Ingredients:

- ½ cup fresh strawberries
- ½ cup plain coconut milk
- 1 tsp honey
- 1 tsp lemon juice

Instructions:

- Mix everything in a blender. Blend well, then serve.

Spinach, Banana, and Flax Protein Smoothie

Introducing our Spinach, Banana, and Flax Protein Smoothie recipe! This healthy and delicious smoothie is packed with nutrients from spinach, banana, and flaxseed, and also provides a boost of protein to keep you feeling full and satisfied. Perfect for a quick breakfast or post-workout snack.

Ingredients:

- 1 cup spinach
- 2 ripe banana
- 1 tbs NutriBullet Organic Pea Protein powder
- 1 tbsp flax seeds
- ½ cup almond milk

Instructions:

- Use a blender to mix everything. Cool and serve.

Pumpkin Ginger Protein Smoothie

Introducing our Pumpkin Ginger Protein Smoothie recipe! This delicious and healthy smoothie is packed with the flavors of pumpkin, ginger, and a boost of protein to keep you satisfied and energized all day. Perfect for a quick and easy breakfast or post-workout snack.

Ingredients:

- 1 cup pumpkin puree
- 1 ripe frozen banana
- ¼ tsp crushed ginger root
- ¼ tsp ground cinnamon
- ¼ tsp vanilla powder

Instructions:

- Use a blender to mix everything. Cool and serve.

Avocado, Spinach, and Kiwi Smoothie

Introducing our Avocado, Spinach, and Kiwi Smoothie recipe! This nutrient-packed smoothie is a great way to start your day, with a delicious blend of healthy fats from avocado, Vitamin C, and antioxidants from kiwi and Spinach, this smoothie is sure to boost your energy and leave you feeling refreshed.

Ingredients:

- 1 cup spinach
- 3 peeled and sliced kiwi
- ½ ripe fresh or frozen avocado
- ½ cup almond or coconut milk
- 3 tbsp organic honey
- 1 cup ice

Instructions:

- Mix all the ingredients until they are smooth. Enjoy!

Chocolate Berry Smoothie

Introducing our Chocolate Berry Smoothie recipe! This delectable and satisfying smoothie is the perfect balance of chocolate and berry flavors, making it a great way to start your day or as a sweet snack. It's easy to make and packed with nutrients, making it a guilt-free indulgence.

Ingredients:

- 2 tsp cocoa powder
- ¾ cup of frozen berries
- 1 ripe banana
- 1 tbsp chia seeds
- 1 cup almond, soy, or coconut milk
- 1tbs honey or maple syrup
- 1 cup ice

Instructions:

- Combine all ingredients and blend to a smooth consistency. Serve immediately.

Strawberry Banana Oatmeal Smoothie

Introducing our Strawberry Banana Oatmeal Smoothie recipe! This delicious and nutritious smoothie is a perfect breakfast or snack option, it's a great way to start the day with a boost of energy and a delicious taste. This recipe is made with fresh strawberries, bananas, and oatmeal, it's rich in antioxidants, vitamins, and minerals. It's easy to make and perfect for busy mornings. Enjoy!

Ingredients:

- ½ cup unsweetened almond milk (I use Silk Pure Almond)
- ½ cup pomegranate juice
- 1 scoop protein powder
- 1 cup packed fresh baby spinach
- ½ banana
- 1 cup frozen strawberries

- ¼ cup old-fashioned rolled oats

Instructions:

- Put the almond milk, pomegranate juice, protein powder, and spinach in a blender and blend until everything is well-mixed.

- Add the banana, strawberries, and oats to the mixture and process again until it is completely smooth. Serve right away.

Berry Spinach Smoothie

This nutritious and delicious smoothie is a perfect blend of fresh berries, spinach, and other ingredients that will give you a boost of energy and provide your body with essential vitamins and minerals. It's easy to make and perfect for a healthy breakfast or snack. Give it a try!

Ingredients:

- 1/2 cup plain Greek Yogurt

- 1/2 cup frozen blueberries

- 1/2 cup frozen cranberries

- 1/2 cup frozen strawberries

- 1/2 frozen banana

- 1-2 large handfuls of spinach

- 1/2-1 cup water (just enough to get everything moving)

Instructions:

- Put the yogurt, spinach, and water in a blender. Then add all the frozen fruit. Blend it until it is smooth, adding more water if you need to.

Peanut Butter and Jelly Protein Smoothie

Introducing our Peanut Butter and Jelly Protein Smoothie recipe! This creamy and satisfying smoothie is a delicious way to fuel your body with the power of protein and the classic flavor of peanut butter and jelly. Perfect for breakfast, lunch, or a post-workout snack.

Ingredients:

- 1 cup mixed frozen berries
- 1-2 tablespoons all-natural peanut butter
- 1/4 cup vanilla protein powder we love Organic Valley*
- 2 tablespoons rolled oats
- 1 cup milk of any kind

Instructions:

- Put all of the ingredients into a blender that works quickly.
- Mix on high until it's smooth.

Mango Carrot Smoothie

Introducing our Mango Carrot Smoothie recipe! This sweet and healthy smoothie combines the tropical taste of mango with the earthy taste of carrots for a

delicious and nutritious drink. Perfect for a morning pick-me-up or post-workout refreshment. Give it a try!

Ingredients:

- 1 ½ cups orange juice
- 1 medium banana
- 1 cup mango chunks
- 1 cup frozen carrots

Instructions:

- Put orange juice, banana, mango, and carrots in the bottom of a blender. Mix until it's smooth.

Tropical Chia Seed Smoothie

A delicious blend of tropical fruits and chia seeds for a boost of nutrients and a taste of the tropics in every sip. Perfect for a refreshing breakfast or a healthy snack on the go.

Ingredients:

- 1 small frozen banana

- ½ cup frozen pineapple chunks

- ½ cup frozen mango chunks

- ½ teaspoon turmeric

- ½ teaspoon minced ginger

- 1½ cups coconut beverage - (not canned), or nondairy milk of choice

- 2 soft Medjool dates - pitted (if not soft, soak in water for 10-15 min)

- 1 tablespoon chia seeds - no need to soak them beforehand

Instructions:

- Put everything in a blender. Start with 1 cup of coconut milk and add more if needed to get the consistency you want. Mix until it's smooth. Pour into a pretty glass with a cool straw, or slice some pineapple or mango to put on the side of the glass.

Detoxing Juices

Green Ginger Ale Weight Loss Juice

This delicious and nutritious juice is packed with leafy greens, ginger, and lemon, making it a great option for those looking to boost their weight loss efforts while also supporting overall health and wellness.

Ingredients:

- 3 medium apples
- 2 stalks celery
- 1 cup spinach
- 1 cucumber
- 1 piece ginger root 1" dia
- 1 lime peeled

Instructions:

- Wash all the ingredients for weight loss juice well and put them in a rat dru.
- Chop fruits and vegetables into 1- to 2-inch pieces. Get rid of any reel.
- Put all of the ingredients in a blender.
- Turn into juice based on what the manufacturer wants.

Lemona

Made with fresh lemons and sweetened to perfection, it's the perfect thirst-quenching drink. This recipe is easy to make and is sure to become a staple in your kitchen. Try it out today!

Ingredients:

- 5 Lemons whole
- 3 Bunch Mint
- 1/2 Cup Honey
- Crushed ice

Instructions:

- Put all the ingredients in a blender with a lot of smashed garlic.
- Cool and serve.

Cucumber Mint Detox Drink

This refreshing and hydrating drink is a perfect way to detoxify and cleanse your body while satisfying your thirst. Cucumber and mint provide a refreshing and cooling taste while also providing a variety of health benefits. It's easy to make and perfect for hot summer days.

Ingredients:

- 1 Cucumber
- 8-10 Mint leaves
- 2 Tbsp Lemon juice
- Ice cubes
- Iced Water
- Lemon rings and mint leaves

Instructions:

- Peel, chop and blend cucumber, mint leaves, and 1 cup of water.
- Strain and discard pulp.
- Add lemon juice, black salt and dilute with water if needed.
- Pour the beverages in glasses, put some ice cubes and garnish with lemon rings and mint leaves.

Pomegranate Juice

Introducing our Pomegranate Juice recipe, a delicious and healthy way to enjoy the benefits of this nutrient-rich fruit. Pomegranate is high in antioxidants and vitamin C, making it a great addition to any juicing routine. Our recipe is easy to make and perfect for a refreshing and healthy drink.

Ingredients:

- 1 Fresh leaf aloe vera
- 1/2 cup Beetroot, chopped
- 2 cups Pomegranate juice or amla juice (Indian gooseberry)
- 1/4 tsp Black pepper powder

Instructions:

- Carefully peel the rind off the aloe vera leaves with a sharp knife and throw away the rind.
- Use a sharp knife to peel off the yellow layer just under the rind. You should be left with about 2 tablespoons (30 ml) of clear aloe vera gel. (Wash the gel off before you put it in the juice.)
- Put chopped beetroot and pomegranate juice in a blender and blend.
- Now add aloe vera gel. Give it a try.
- Lastlu add some blask pepper and serve.

Radiant Lemonade

This zesty and refreshing juice is made with fresh lemons and is the perfect way to quench your thirst on a hot summer day. Perfectly balanced with sweetness, tanginess, and hydrating properties, this juice

recipe is a must-try for anyone who loves a good lemonade.

Ingredients:

- 1 apple, chopped
- 1 carrot, chopped
- 1/2 beetroot, sliced
- 2-3 slices white radish
- 1/2 tsp lemon zest
- 2 lemons (juiced)

Instructions:

- Blend all the ingredients in a blender.
- Adjust the soy sauce by adding a little bit of water.
- Sift and sift.

Ginger Litchi Lemonade

This zesty and flavorful juice combines the sweetness of litchi, the tang of lemon, and the heat of ginger for a refreshing and unique taste experience. Perfect for a hot summer day or as an immune booster. Give it a try and enjoy the benefits of this delicious juice.

Ingredients:

- 1/2 cup ginger (minced)
- 1/2 cup fresh lemon juice
- Ice cubes (as needed)
- 1 glass lychee juice
- 1 cup grapes
- 1/2 cup chia seeds
- Mint leaves
- A pinch of salt

Instructions:

- In a jar, put minced ginger, lemon juice and lychee juice.
- Add some ice, salt to taste and blend it well.
- Pour it in a jar. Add sliced grapes and chia seeds to it. Mix it well with a spoon.
- Finally garnish it with some mint leaves and serve chilled.

Aam Panna

This traditional Indian recipe is made with raw mango, mint, and spices for a refreshing and tangy summer drink. Perfect for beating the heat and keeping your body hydrated.

Ingredients:

- 500 gm green mangoes
- 1/2 cup sugar
- 2 tsp salt
- 2 tsp kala namak (black rock salt)
- 2 tsp roasted and powdered cumin seeds
- 2 Tbsp finely chopped mint leaves
- 2 cups water

Instructions:

- Boil the mangoes until they get soft on the inside and their skin turns brown.

- When the mango is cool enough to touch, peel off the skin and squeeze the pulp out.
- Mix all the ingredients, blend, and then add 2 cups of water.
- Put someone in each glass and then pour the ranna on top.

Detox Haldi Tea

This unique and flavorful juice is made with turmeric, ginger, lemon, and honey to help detoxify the body, boost the immune system, and promote overall health and wellness.

Ingredients:

- 1/2 tsp haldi
- 1/2 tsp ginger, chopped
- 1/4 tsp black Pepper
- 1 tsp honey
- 2 cups water

Instructions:

- Put water in a bowl and heat it.

- Bring it and all the other ingredients to a low boil.
- Stir well.
- Keep boiling the water until it's half as much as it was before.
- Give hot food.

Honey Lemon Ginger Tea

This warm and comforting juice is a perfect blend of sweet honey, tangy lemon, and spicy ginger, which makes it perfect for a cold day and also helps to boost the immune system. A delicious and healthy way to warm up!

Ingredients:

- 3 Cups Water
- 1 tsp Ginger, finely chopped
- 1 tsp Tea leaves, for every cup
- 1 tsp Lemon juice
- 1 tsp Honey

Instructions:

- Before the water starts to boil, add the ginger to the pan.
- Just as it starts to boil, add the tea leaves, lemon juice, and honey.
- Strain it into a cup and enjoy!

Coconut Water with Lemon and Mint

This refreshing and hydrating juice is a perfect way to cool down on a hot day and is packed with natural electrolytes, vitamins, and minerals. This recipe is easy to make and perfect for anyone looking for a healthy, thirst-quenching drink.

Ingredients:

- 1 coconut
- Mint leaves
- 1 tbsp honey
- 1 lemon

Instructions:

- Break open a coconut and pour water into a jug. Scoop out the meat of the coconut with a spoon. Chop it up and add it to the coconut water.
- Add mint, honey, and lemon juise as well as lemon.
- Stir well, mix, and serve.

Tropical Mint

This refreshing and flavorful juice combines tropical fruits like pineapple and mango with the cool and invigorating taste of mint for a perfect summertime drink. Perfect to enjoy as a morning boost or after a workout. This recipe is easy to make and packed with vitamins and minerals.

Ingredients:

- 2 stalks celery
- 1/2 cucumber
- 2 cups spinach
- 3 cups mint leaves
- 1 cup pineapple

- 1/2 lemon

Instructions:

- Put all the ingredients in your juicer and serve it cold.

Ginger Zinger

This tangy and spicy juice is made with fresh ginger, lemon, and apples, perfect for a morning boost or a post-workout refreshment. It's a great way to add a little zing to your day!

Ingredients:

- 2 stalks celery
- ½ cucumber
- 1½ cm ginger
- ½ cup parsley
- ½ lemon
- 1 green apple
- 2 cups spinach

Instructions:

- Place all ingredients into your juicer.

- Serve with ice.ù

Beet-It-Up

This vibrant and nutritious juice is made with fresh beets, ginger, and other seasonal fruits and vegetables for a powerful boost of antioxidants, minerals, and energy. Perfect as a breakfast or post-workout drink, it's a great way to start your day or refresh yourself. Get ready to Beet-It-Up!

Ingredients:

- 1½ cm fresh ginger
- 3 beets
- 3 carrots
- 3 stalks celery

Instructions:

- Put all of the ingredients in the juicer.
- Serve with ice.

Kale + Pear

Kale + Pear juice is a refreshing and popular drink that can be enjoyed by anyone. Kale + pear juice is high in antioxidants and contains key nutrients that are beneficial for the body. It is also known to be a healthy choice for those looking for an energy boost.

Ingredients:

- 2 stalks kale
- 1 cup spinach
- 1 pear
- ½ lime
- 3 stalks celery
- ½ cucumber

Instructions:

- Place all ingredients into your juiser.
- Serve with ice.

Tumeric Tonic

Tumeric is a natural drink that has been used in many different recipes throughout history. Today, it is still a popular drink in many parts of the world and can be found in most grocery stores. Tumeric is a key ingredient in many tonic recipes and can be used to provide a refreshing taste.

Ingredients:

- 2 cups coconut water (like this) (or filtered water)
- 2 tbsp grated fresh turmeric (or 1/2 to 1 tsp dried turmeric powder)
- 1 tbsp grated fresh ginger
- juice from 1 lemon or orange
- 1 medium carrot
- 1 tbsp raw honey (like this) or real maple syrup (like this)
- pinch of black pepper

- Optional: a pinch of cayenne or cinnamon

Instructions:

- Put all of the ingredients into a high-speed blender and mix them until they are smooth. Drink as is or strain before serving.

Electric Green

Electric green juice is a healthy drink that can help you lose weight and improve your health. It is made from natural ingredients and has no sugar or calorie content. You can make it at home with just a few simple ingredients

Ingredients:

- 1 cucumber
- 1 cup parsley
- 1 cup spinach
- 2 green apples

Instructions:

- Place all ingredients into your juiser.
- Serve with ice.

Summer Juice

This is a perfect juice recipe to enjoy either alone or with friends and family. It improves mood and creates a happy atmosphere.

Ingredients:

- 1 cup pineapple
- ½ lemon
- 2 carrots
- 2 stalks celery
- 1 cm ginger

Instructions:

- Put all of the ingredients in your juicer.
- Serve with ice.

Cilantro

Cilantro juice is a great mix of amazing vegetables that helps build the immune system and keeps us refreshed.

Ingredients:

- 2 stalks celery
- ½ cucumber
- ½ lime
- 1 cup cilantro
- 1 cup kale
- 1 green apple

Instructions:

- Put everything into your juicer.
- Serve with ice.

Carrot Cleanser

Carrot Cleanser Juice is a simple and healthy juice recipe made with fresh carrots, apples, ginger, and lemon. The natural sweetness of the carrots and apples is balanced by the zing of ginger and lemon, making it a refreshing and energizing drink. It is a great way to incorporate more veggies into your diet and support your overall health and well-being.

Ingredients:

- 4 carrots
- 1 cm fresh ginger
- 1 green apple

Instructions:

- Place all ingredients into your juicer.
- Use cold food.

Sweet Beet

This refreshing drink is made with fresh beets, carrots, ginger, and a hint of lemon. It's packed with vitamins, minerals, and antioxidants, making it the perfect addition to your daily routine. This recipe is easy to make, and it's a great way to incorporate more beets into your diet. Enjoy!

Ingredients:

- 1 beet
- 2 carrots
- 3 stalks celery
- ½ lemon
- 1 cm ginger
- 1 green apple

Instructions:

- Place all ingredients into your juicer.
- Serve with ice.

Vegetable Juices

Cucumber Juice

Cucumber juice is a refreshing and hydrating drink that is easy to make at home. It is made by blending fresh cucumbers and adding a touch of lemon juice and honey for flavor. This recipe is a great way to incorporate more cucumbers into your diet and is perfect for a summer day.

Ingredients:

- 1 cucumber
- Juice of 1/2 lemon
- 1/4 teaspoon black salt

Instructions:

- Cut the cucumber into small pieces and put them in the blender.
- Spin it around.
- Fill a glass with cucumber juice.
- Add lemon juice and black salt. Stir well.

Celery Juice

It is made by blending celery with water and a little bit of lemon juice. This juice is packed with vitamins and minerals, making it a great way to boost your health and energy levels. Whether you're looking for a refreshing morning pick-me-up or a post-workout boost, celery juice is a perfect choice.

Ingredients:

- 2 celery stalks
- A handful of coriander leaves
- Juice of 1/2 lemon
- A pinch of black or pink salt

Instructions:

- Cut the celery stalks into small pieces and put them in the blender.
- Add the coriander leaves and stir them around.
- Put the juice of the celery into a glass.

- Add some salt and lemon juice. Stir well.

Cabbage Juice

Cabbage juice is a delicious and healthy beverage that can be enjoyed at any time of the day. It is packed with vitamins and minerals and is a great way to boost your immune system and improve your overall health. This recipe is easy to make and only requires a few simple ingredients. Give it a try and see for yourself how delicious and nutritious it can be!

Ingredients:

- 1 cup chopped cabbage
- 1 cup chopped cucumber
- 1/2 teaspoon black salt
  Juice of 1/2 lemon

Instructions:

- Put the chopped cabbage and cucumber in the blender. Test it out.
- Put some of the juice in a glass.
- Add lemon juice and black salt. Stir well.

Beetroot Juice

Beetroot juice is a delicious and nutritious drink made by blending fresh beetroot with water and other ingredients such as ginger, lemon, or apple. It is a great way to boost your energy and improve your overall health. This recipe is simple and easy to make and can be enjoyed as a morning juice or as a post-workout drink.

Ingredients:

- 1 beetroot
- 1/2 teaspoon roasted cumin powder
- Juice of 1/4 lemon

- A pinch of salt

Instructions:

- Cut the beets into small pieces and put them in the blender. Test it out.
- Pour the juice from the beetroots into a glass.
- Add salt, roasted cumin powder, and lemon juice. Stir well.

Bitter Gourd Juice

Bitter Gourd Juice is a nutritious and refreshing drink made from bitter gourd vegetables. It's a great way to incorporate the health benefits of bitter gourd into your diet and can be enjoyed both as a standalone drink and as an ingredient in other recipes. This recipe is easy to make and can be customized to your taste preferences.

Ingredients:

- 1 bitter gourd

- A pinch of salt

Instructions:

- Cut the bitter gourd into small pieces and throw them into the blender. Test it out.
- Pour the juice from the bitter gourd into a glass.
- Add salt and stir well.

Wheatgrass Juice

Wheatgrass juice is a nutrient-rich drink made from the freshly juiced leaves of the wheat plant. It is packed with vitamins, minerals, antioxidants, and enzymes, making it a powerful superfood for promoting overall health and wellness. This recipe for wheatgrass juice is easy to make and can be enjoyed on its own or added to other juices and smoothies for an extra boost of nutrition.

Ingredients:

- 1 cup chopped wheatgrass
- Juice of 1/4 lemon
- A pinch of black salt

Instructions:

- Put the wheatgrass in the blender for about 30 seconds.
- Pour the juice through a strainer into a glass.
- Add lemon and black salt. Stir well.

Aloe Vera Juice

Aloe vera juice is a refreshing and nutritious drink that is easy to make at home. Made from the sap of the aloe vera plant, this juice is packed with vitamins, minerals, and antioxidants that can help boost your immune system and improve your overall health. Whether you're looking to detoxify your body or just want a delicious and healthy beverage, this recipe is a perfect choice.

Ingredients:

- 1 aloe vera leaf
- Juice of 1/4 lemon
- A pinch of salt

Instructions:

- Peel and chop the aloe vera leaf. Throw everything into the blender and turn it on.
- Pour the juice of aloe vera into a glass.
- Add some salt and lemon juice. Stir well.

Twitter Bitter

Introducing our Twitter Bitter Juice recipe, a perfect blend of bitter and sweet flavors that is sure to tantalize your taste buds. This unique recipe combines the tangy taste of fresh citrus with the bitter kick of Campari, making for a refreshing and irresistible drink. Perfect for sipping on a hot summer day or enjoying a cocktail party, this recipe is sure to be a hit with your friends and family.

Ingredients:

- 1 bitter gourd
- 1-inch aloe vera leaf
- 1-inch cucumber
- A pinch of salt
- A pinch of cayenne pepper

Instructions:

- Wash the bitter gourd, cut it in half, and take the seeds out of each half.
- Cut the aloe vera leaf open and take the gel out.
- Bitter gourd and cucumber should be cut into small cubes.
- Mix the bitter gourd, cucumber, and aloe vera. Add a pinch of salt and cayenne pepper. Stir well and drink.

Tomato and Cucumber Juice

This recipe is for a refreshing and healthy juice made from tomatoes and cucumbers. It's a great way to get your daily dose of vitamins and minerals, and it's easy to make with just a few simple ingredients.

Ingredients:

- 1 cup chopped cucumber
- 1/2 cup chopped tomato
- 1/4 lemon juice
- A pinch of salt

Instructions:

- Put the chopped tomato and cucumber in the blender and turn it on.
- Add some salt and lemon juice. Stir well.

Celery and Beet Juice

This Celery and Beet Juice recipe is a delicious and healthy way to start your day. Packed with vitamins and minerals, it's the perfect way to boost your energy and get your body moving. With just a few simple ingredients, you can enjoy this refreshing juice in no time.

Ingredients:

- 2 celery stalks
- 1/2 cup chopped beetroot
- Coriander leaves for garnishing
- A pinch of salt

Instructions:

- Cut the celery stalks into small pieces and put them in the blender.
- Put the pieces of beetroot in the blender and turn them on.
- Add a pinch of salt to the juice in a glass.
- Give it a good stir and top it with coriander leaves.

Broccoli and Green Grapes Juice

This Broccoli and Green Grapes Juice recipe is a delicious and healthy way to get your daily dose of vitamins and nutrients. The combination of broccoli and grapes provides a unique taste and a boost of antioxidants. Perfect for a morning pick-me-up or a refreshing post-workout drink.

Ingredients:

- 1/2 cup broccoli
- 1/2 cup green grapes
- A pinch of black pepper
- A pinch of salt

Instructions:

- Put the green grapes and broccoli in a blender and give it a spin.

- Pour the juice through a strainer into a glass.
- Add a pinch of salt and black pepper. Stir well.

Honeydew Melon and Cucumber Crush

This delicious combination of sweet honeydew melon and cool cucumber is perfect for a hot summer day. It's easy to make and packed with vitamins and minerals. Give it a try and enjoy the taste of summer with every sip!

Ingredients:

- 1 cup honeydew melon
- 1/2 cup cucumber
- 1/4 cup ice water
- A handful of mint leaves
- A pinch of black salt

Instructions:

- Toss the honeydew melon, cucumber, ice water, and mint leaves into a blender and give it a spin.
- Pour the juice into a glass.
- Add a pinch of black salt and stir well.

Bottle Gourd & Watermelon Juice

This Bottle of Gourd & Watermelon Juice recipe is a refreshing and healthy way to start your day. Made with fresh bottle gourd and watermelon, it's packed with vitamins and minerals that will energize you and help you stay hydrated. It's easy to make and can be enjoyed any time of the day. Give it a try and see for yourself!

Ingredients:

- 1 cup shredded bottle of gourd
- 1 cup watermelon
- A handful of coriander leaves
- A pinch of roasted cumin powder

- A pinch of black salt

Instructions:

- Put the bottle of gourd, watermelon, and coriander leaves in a blender and give it a spin.
- Pour the juice through a strainer into a glass.
- Add a pinch of roasted cumin powder and black salt. Stir well.

Leek and Broccoli Juice

This Leek and Broccoli Juice recipe is a healthy and delicious way to get your daily dose of vitamins and minerals. The combination of leek and broccoli provides a rich source of antioxidants and anti-inflammatory compounds, making it a perfect addition to any diet. With its refreshing taste and easy preparation, this juice is sure to become a favorite.

Ingredients:

- 1/2 cup chopped leek
- 1 cup broccoli
- A pinch of black pepper
- A pinch of salt
- A dash of lime juice

Instructions:

- Mix the leek and broccoli.
- Pour the juice through a strainer into a glass.
- Sprinkle some salt and pepper on it.
- Pour in the lime juice and mix it up well.

Pear and Spinach Juice

This Pear and Spinach Juice recipe is a refreshing and healthy way to start your day. Made with fresh pears and spinach, it is packed with vitamins and antioxidants to give you a boost of energy. It's easy to make and only takes a few minutes to prepare. Give it a try and enjoy the benefits of this delicious and nutritious juice.

Ingredients:

- 1 pear
- 1 cup spinach
- 1/2 teaspoon apple cider vinegar
- 1/2 cup ice water
- A pinch of salt

Instructions:

- Chop the pear into small pieces and put them in the blender.
- Put the spinach and ice water in the pan. Test it out.
- Pour the juice through a strainer into a glass.
- Add apple cider vinegar and salt. Stir well.

Healthy Green Vegetable Juice

This refreshing juice is packed with vitamins and minerals from a variety of green vegetables, making it the perfect way to start your day or boost your energy throughout the day. With simple ingredients and easy instructions, this recipe is a great way to incorporate more greens into your diet. So, grab your juicer, and let's get started!

Ingredients:

- 4 oz cucumber
- 4 oz celery
- 4 oz kale
- 1.5 cups apple juice (16 oz apple)
- 0.3 cup mint leaves
- 4 tsp lemon juice
- 4 tsp honey

Instructions:

- Put the ingredients in a juicer and get the juice from it.
- Pour the juice into a pitcher and put it on the table. Refrigerate for at least 1 hour before serving if desired (best if drunk within 24 hours).

Tomato-Vegetable Juice

This Tomato-Vegetable Juice recipe is a delicious and healthy way to start your day. Made with fresh tomatoes, carrots, celery, and a hint of ginger, this juice is packed with vitamins and nutrients to keep you feeling energized and refreshed. It's easy to make and can be customized to your taste preferences. Perfect for a quick breakfast or a healthy snack.

Ingredients:

- 1 cup chopped hearts of romaine
- ¼ cup chopped fresh chives
- 2 large tomatoes, cut into wedges
- 1/4 fresh jalapeño, stemmed and seeded
- 1 large red bell pepper, cut into eighths
- 2 large stalks of celery, trimmed
- 1 medium carrot, peeled
- Ice cubes

Instructions:

- Put the ingredients in a juicer and get the juice from it.
- Pour the juice into a pitcher and put it on the table. Refrigerate for at least 1 hour before serving if desired (best if drunk within 24 hours).

Spinach-Apple Juice

This Spinach-Apple Juice recipe is a refreshing and healthy drink that is perfect for any time of the day. With the combination of fresh spinach and sweet apples, this juice is packed with vitamins and minerals that will give you a boost of energy and help you stay on track with your health goals. It is easy to make and requires only a few simple ingredients. Give it a try and enjoy the delicious taste and benefits of this green juice!

Ingredients:

- 1 ½ cups spinach
- ½ grapefruit, peeled, white pith removed
- 2 green apples, cut into eighths
- 1 1-inch pieces peeled fresh ginger
- 2 large stalks of celery
- Ice (optional)

Instructions:

- Follow the instructions for your juicer to put spinach, grapefruit, apples, ginger, and celery through it in this order. (No juicer? See Blender Variation.)
- If you want, put ice in two glasses and pour the juice into them. Serve right away.

Blueberry-Cabbage Power Juice

Introducing our Blueberry-Cabbage Power Juice recipe - a delicious and nutritious blend of sweet blueberries and nutrient-rich cabbage. Perfect for a morning boost or post-workout refuel, this juice is packed with vitamins and antioxidants to help keep you feeling energized and refreshed. So grab your blender and let's get juicing!

Ingredients:

- ¼ medium red cabbage, sliced
- 1 large cucumber, peeled and cut into chunks
- 1 cup fresh blueberries
- 1 large apple, cut into eighths
- Ice cubes (optional)

Instructions:

- Follow the instructions for your juicer to put cabbage, cucumber, blueberries, and apple through it in this order.

- If you want, put ice in two glasses and then pour the juice into the glasses. Serve right away.

Strawberry-Cucumber Juice

This Strawberry-Cucumber Juice recipe is a refreshing and healthy beverage that combines the sweet taste of strawberries with the crispness of cucumbers. It's a perfect drink for a hot summer day or as a pre-workout boost. With just a few simple ingredients, it's easy to make and packed with vitamins and antioxidants. Enjoy!

Ingredients:

- 6 fresh strawberries, hulled

- 1 large cucumber, peeled and cut into chunks

- 1 large red apple, cut into eighths

- 2 medium carrots, peeled

- Ice (optional)

Instructions:

- Working in this order process strawberries, cucumber, apple, and carrots through a juicer according to the manufacturer's directions. (No juicer? Blender Variation.)

- Fill 2 glasses with ice, if desired, and pour the juice into the glasses. Serve immediately.

Antiaging Juices

Island Lime Collagen Colada Smoothie

Introducing the Island Lime Collagen Colada Smoothie - a tropical and refreshing blend of coconut milk, lime juice, pineapple, and collagen powder. Perfect for a healthy breakfast or post-workout snack.

Ingredients:

- 1 cup cashew milk (or milk of choice)
- 1 cup cold water
- 1 lime, cut into ⅛'s
- ½ frozen banana
- ¼ cup shredded coconut, unsweetened
- ¼ cup macadamia nuts, unsalted
- ¼ cup frozen pineapple
- zest and juice of additional lime
- 1 scoop Further Food Premium Marine Collagen
- 1 to 2 cups of ice

Instructions:

- Place cashew milk, water, and lime segments into the blender and pulse 4-5 times to coarsely chop but not completely pulverize. Strain through a fine mesh sieve into a clean bowl, rinse the blender out, and pour "lime-infused" milk back into it.

- Add remaining ingredients and blend until the consistency you want is reached. Add as much or little ice as you like. More ice will give you a thicker consistency, possibly requiring a straw! Whereas less ice will make it more "sip-able" ~~ either way, find a great spot to take a few minutes for yourself and escape away for a few minutes to the islands!

Matcha Latte

Matcha Latte is a delicious and healthy drink that combines the earthy flavor of matcha powder with the creamy texture of steamed milk. This recipe is easy to make and is a perfect way to start your day or as a pick-me-up during the afternoon.

Ingredients:

- 1 teaspoon Superfood Matcha
- ¼ cup hot water
- 1 cup milk of choice (we used unsweetened vanilla almond milk)
- 1 teaspoon honey or sweetener of choice (we used stevia)

Instructions:

- Mix Superfood Matcha into hot water in a large mug.
- Whisk vigorously with a bamboo whisk or spoon until frothy.
- Heat milk and whisk vigorously. Stir in the desired sweetener.
- Pour milk into the tea mug and enjoy!

Turmeric Piña Colada Smoothie (Dairy-Free, Gluten-Free)

Introducing our delicious Turmeric Piña Colada Smoothie - a dairy-free and gluten-free twist on the classic tropical drink. This smoothie combines the anti-inflammatory benefits of turmeric with the refreshing taste of pineapple and coconut for a healthy and tasty treat. Perfect for a summertime pick-me-up or a post-workout recovery drink. Give it a try!

Ingredients:

- 1 cup frozen pineapple (diced)
- 1/4 frozen banana
- 3/4 cup coconut milk
- 1 teaspoon honey (optional)

- 1 teaspoon Further Food Superfood Turmeric
- 1/4 teaspoon cinnamon (plus additional for topping)
- 1 teaspoon shredded coconut

Instructions:

- Add all ingredients to a blender (or immersion blender) and blend for 3-4 minutes (depending on how you like the texture of your smoothie)
- Serve in glasses and top with cinnamon and shredded coconut.

Watermelon Berry Blast Smoothie

This Watermelon Berry Blast Smoothie is the perfect refreshment on a hot summer day. Made with fresh watermelon, mixed berries, and yogurt, it's a delicious and healthy way to cool down.

Ingredients:

- 4 c. Watermelon, one-inch cubes
- 2 cups cucumber, one-inch cubes
- Juice of one lime
- 1/2 cup Blueberries, frozen
- 1/3 cup Almond milk
- 1 T. Chia seeds
- 2 drops Stevia
- 2 cups Ice.

Instructions:

- Add all the ingredients to your blender and mix on high until smooth and frothy.

Homemade Anti-Aging Citrus Juice

Introducing our Homemade Anti-Aging Citrus Juice recipe, a delicious and healthy way to boost your skin's collagen production and fight the signs of aging. Made with a combination of citrus fruits, ginger, and turmeric, this juice is packed with antioxidants, vitamins, and minerals that will leave your skin looking and feeling youthful. So why not give it a try and see the difference for yourself!

Ingredients:

- 10 Mandarins
- 5 Oranges
- 1 Grapefruit
- ½ Lemon
- ¼ Lime
- Agave Syrup to taste (optional)

Instructions:

- Rinse all the fruits under running water. Peel mandarins, oranges, and grapefruit. Juice them. Squeeze in lemon and lime.
- Taste it and sweeten it with agave syrup if you feel like it is needed!

Anti-Aging Beet Grape Juice

Made with the power of beets and grapes, this juice is packed with antioxidants and anti-inflammatory properties that can help fight the signs of aging and keep your skin looking youthful and radiant. Perfect for a morning boost or an afternoon pick-me-up, this juice is easy to make and will leave you feeling refreshed and rejuvenated. So, give your skin the gift of youth and try our Anti-Aging Beet Grape Juice today!

Ingredients:

- 2 cups red grapes
- 4 celery stalks
- 4 beets (beetroot), optional to include beet leaves
- 4 large carrots

Instructions:

- Wash all produce well.

- Peel the beets and remove grapes from the stem.

- Add all ingredients through a juicer and enjoy.

Mango Kale Smoothie with Collagen

This smoothie is a perfect blend of sweet mango, nutrient-rich kale, and collagen for an added boost of protein and amino acids. Perfect for a quick breakfast or post-workout snack. Give it a try and see for yourself!

Ingredients:

- 1 cup (67 g) chopped kale - frozen (the fresh bagged kind from the produce section, brought home and tossed in the freezer), tightly packed

- ¾ cup (124 g) frozen mango chunks - from the frozen section

- ¾ cup (177 g) frozen pineapple chunks - from the frozen section

- 1 tablespoon (15 ml) apple cider vinegar - unfiltered, with "the mother"

- 20 g collagen peptides - 2 scoops

- 2 tablespoons (14 g) ground flaxseeds

- 1 cup (250 g) water or almond milk - plus more if needed

Instructions:

- Add all ingredients to the blender, keeping kale closest to the cutting blades and being sure not to go over your blender cup's liquid fill line.

- Blend until kale is fully puréed and mixture is smooth.

- Divide into two glasses and serve!

Delicious Mash

Introducing our Delicious Mash Juice recipe - a combination of fresh fruits and vegetables blended to perfection, creating a nutritious and tasty drink that will leave you feeling refreshed and energized. Perfect for a healthy breakfast or a mid-day pick-me-up, this recipe is easy to make and can be tailored to your taste preferences. Give it a try and experience the deliciousness of homemade mash juice!

Ingredients:

- Cucumber juice – ¼ cup
- Carrot juice – ¼ cup
- Apple Juice – 1 cup
- Kale juice – ¾ cup
- Organic plain Yoghurt – ¼ cup

Instructions:

- Combine all the juices and mix them well. Add the yogurt to it and blend it. Add some ice and drink chilled. Try to use fresh juices as fresh ingredients will work better.

Apple and Blueberry Juice

"This recipe for Apple and Blueberry Juice is a refreshing and healthy option for any time of day. Made with fresh apples and blueberries, it's packed with vitamins and antioxidants. It's easy to make and perfect for a quick breakfast or a refreshing afternoon drink."

Ingredients:

- Blueberries – 2 cups
- Apples – 2

Instructions:

- Thoroughly wash and remove the seeds of the fruits. Put them in a blender and make juice. Add some ice and enjoy this tasty drink. Drink the juice immediately after preparation; it will gain a gel-like texture after half an hour of preparation.

Cucumber Juice

Cucumber Juice is a refreshing and healthy drink that is easy to make and packed with nutrients. This recipe uses fresh cucumbers, lemon, and mint to create a delicious and hydrating beverage that is perfect for hot summer days. With just a few simple ingredients and a blender, you can enjoy this tasty juice in no time.

Ingredients:

- Cucumber – 1
- Carrots – 2
- Apples – 2
- Celery stalk – 1

Instructions:

- Use the whole cucumber as it is, without peeling. Most of the silicon in cucumber is found in the skin itself. Combine all the ingredients and blend them. Drink with ice.

Drinking this juice regularly will help to reduce wrinkles.

Mango, Cucumber and Spinach Smoothie

This refreshing Mango, Cucumber, and Spinach Smoothie is the perfect way to start your day. With a blend of sweet mango, cool cucumber, and nutrient-rich spinach, this smoothie is packed with vitamins and minerals to give you a boost of energy and keep you feeling full until lunchtime.

Ingredients:

- Mango – 1/2 Cup
- Cucumber – 1
- Spinach – Handful

Instructions:

- Peel and mash the flesh of the ripe mango, peel the cucumber, chop the spinach and add all the fruits and vegetables to the food processor. Blend it for a few minutes, pour it in a tall glass, and enjoy this delicious smoothie.

Cantaloupes, Carrots, and Celery Smoothie

Try this out and thank me later.

Ingredients:

- Cantaloupe Slices – 3 to 4
- Carrots – 3
- Celery Stalk – 2

Instructions:

- Cut the cantaloupes and carrots into medium-sized cubes, chop the celery and put all the ingredients into the food processor. Pour 1/2 cup of water and mash it for a few minutes to have your rejuvenating skin detox juice.

Lettuce, Mint, and Cucumber Smoothie

A perfect combination for an amazing juice recipe

Ingredients:

- Cucumbers – 3
- Romaine Lettuce – 1 small head
- Mint Leaves – A Handful
- Lemon Juice – 2 Tablespoons

Instructions:

- Peel and chop the cucumber along with the lettuce and mint leaves, add all the ingredient in the food processer along with 1/2 cup of water, blend well, and add the lemon juice to it, pour in a tall serving glass and enjoy with a few ice cubes.

Apple, Strawberry, and Kale Smoothie

An awesome juicing recipe to try out.

Ingredients:

- Apple – 1
- Strawberries – 2 Cups
- Kale – 6 Leaves

Instructions:

- Deseed the apple and chop the strawberries and kale. Take all the fruits and vegetables in a food processor along with 1/4th cup water and blend well to form a paste of smooth consistency. Pour it into a tall mug and enjoy.

Orange, Broccoli, and Water Cress Smoothie

This an awesome juicing recipe to try!

Ingredients:

- Oranges – 3
- Broccoli – 1 Cup
- Watercress – 1 Handful

Instructions:

- Chop the broccoli into small pieces and take 1 cup of it, chop the watercress, peel the oranges and put all the ingredients in a food processor. Blend till it forms a smooth paste and enjoys in a tall serving glass.

Beets, Cucumber and Red Apple Smoothie

An awesome juicing recipe to try out.

Ingredients:

- Beets Roots – 2
- Red Apple – 1
- Cucumber – 1

Instructions:

- Wash and peel the beetroots and cucumbers, chop all the

components and put them in the food processor, add ½ cup of water to it and mix well till it forms a smooth paste. Enjoy with a sprinkle of chia seed powder from the top.

Sweet Potato, Spinach, and Ginger Smoothie

Mash these together to create a sweet, and gingery taste Juice.

Ingredients:

- Sweet Potato – 2
- Spinach – A Handful
- Ginger – 1-Inch Piece

Instructions:

- Wash and peel the sweet potatoes and cut them into medium-sided cubes. Chop the spinach and add all the constituents in the food processor along with ½ cup of water and blend for a few minutes

to form a smooth paste, pour it in a serving mug, and enjoy.

Pineapple, Cucumber, and Parsley Smoothie

This is a perfect combination for an excellent juice. You can't go wrong with these three recipes.

Ingredients:

- Pineapple – 1 Cup
- Parsley – A Handful
- Cucumber – 1

Instructions:

- Roughly chop the pineapples, cucumber, and parsley, and put all the ingredients in the food processor. Add 1/2 cup of water to it and blend thoroughly. Pour in a tall serving glass and enjoy the refreshing smoothie.

Cabbage, Cucumber, and Carrots Smoothie

With a mixture of cabbage, carrot, and cucumber, you can create an amazing and healthy juice for you and your loved ones.

Ingredients:

- Cabbage Leaves – 6 Large
- Carrots – 2
- Cucumber -1

Instructions:

- Wash and chop the cabbage leaves, carrots, and cucumber. Put them in the food processor and add ½ cup of water to it. Blend till all the vegetables turn into a smooth paste. Pour in a tumbler and enjoy with a dash of lemon juice.

Pear, Lemon, and Cucumber Smoothie

Amazing recipe to change your juicing game.

Ingredients:

- Pears – 2 Large
- Cucumber – 1
- Lemon – 1

Instructions:

- Peel the pears and chop into medium-sized cubes after removing the seeds, chop the cucumber and add both ingredients to the blender. Squeeze in the juice of 1 lemon and blend well. Pour in a tall serving glass and enjoy with ice.

The 6-Weeks Shred Program

Conclusion

In conclusion, juicing is a fantastic way to nourish your body with the vitamins, minerals, and antioxidants found in fruits and vegetables. The juice extraction process makes it easier for your body to absorb and utilize these nutrients, making juicing a great way to support your overall health and wellness.

The recipes in this book offer a wide variety of options for all tastes and dietary needs, and they are all easy to make at home with a good juicer. Whether you are a beginner or an experienced juicer, we hope you have found some new and exciting recipes to try. The different combinations of fruits and vegetables in each recipe not only deliver great taste but also offer a balance of nutrients that will help to support your immune system, improve digestion and promote overall well-being.

We also encourage you to experiment and come up with your unique recipes. Juicing allows you to be creative and come up with your combination of fruits and vegetables that cater to your taste buds and dietary needs. Remember to always use fresh, high-quality ingredients and listen to your body to find the right balance of fruits and vegetables for your needs.

In addition to providing essential nutrients, juicing can also be a great tool for weight management, as it can help to curb cravings for processed foods and sugary snacks. Incorporating juicing into your daily routine can be a simple and enjoyable way to improve your overall health and well-being.

It's important to note that juicing should not replace whole fruits and vegetables and it's always better to consume whole fruits and vegetables than just juice. And also it's important to check with a doctor before making any significant changes to your diet.

You can experiment with different ingredients and ratios to find a combination that you like. Keep in mind, drinking a glass of juice is a great way to start your day but it's not enough to fulfill all your daily nutritional needs, it's always recommended to combine it with a balanced diet and a healthy lifestyle.

All the ingredients used here are easy to find and use. You only need at most 10 minutes or less out of your day to make any of these amazing meal replacement smoothie recipes.

In summary, juicing is a delicious and convenient way to boost your nutrient intake, support your immune system, and improve your overall health. We hope that this book has inspired you to start juicing and making it a regular part of your daily routine. So start getting fit, healthy, and focused with your smoothie of choice.

Happy juicing!

Made in the USA
Coppell, TX
17 April 2023